COTTON

INVESTIGATE MATERIALS

Contents

HOW TO USE THIS BOOK

Before reading with your child it will be helpful to look through the book together and talk about the cover, pictures, and new challenge words. This story is called cotton. Let's read the book to find out about cotton, where it comes from, and how we use it.

Challenge Words

cotton: the thread made from the cotton plant, used to make cotton fabric.

material: something used to make fabric or other items.

fabric: cloth.

seed pod: the shell or case around a seed.

cotton gin: a machine that cleans seeds from cotton.

thread: a long, thin piece of cotton, nylon, or other material used to knit or weave fabric.

dye: to change the color of something.

weave: to push strands of thread over and under rows of thread to make fabric.

knit: to make loops of thread and join the loops to make fabric.

pattern: a design that repeats over and over, such as stripes.

durable: able to last a long time.

denim: a strong cotton fabric used to make jeans.

What is cotton?

Cotton is a **material**. A material is used to make something. We use cotton to make **fabric**.

Where does cotton come from?

Cotton comes from a
cotton plant. The cotton
plant grows in places
where the weather is warm.

Cotton grows inside a **seed pod**. When the cotton gets big and fluffy, it bursts out of the pod.

How is cotton made into fabric?

Farmers use a cotton picker to pick cotton. At first cotton has lots of seeds, sticks, and leaves in it. A machine called a **cotton gin** cleans the dirty cotton.

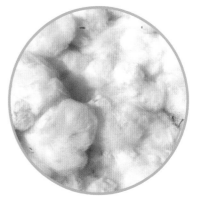

The clean cotton is combed to make it smooth. Then it is twisted into **thread**. The thread can be **dyed** different colors.

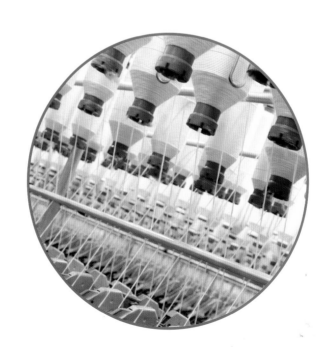

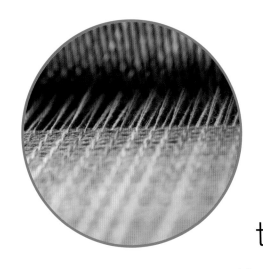

Cotton thread is ready to **weave** or **knit** into fabric. Weaving is pushing thread over and under other threads.

This makes a **pattern**.

Knitting is making loops of thread and joining them.

What does cotton look like?

A cotton ball looks like fluffy white cotton candy. That's how "cotton candy" got its name! A thread of cotton looks like a twisted ribbon.

How does cotton feel?

Cotton is soft. It feels cozy against your skin. When you wear clothes made out of cotton, you feel happy!

Why do we use cotton?

Cotton is easy to grow and make into fabric. It is comfortable to wear. And cotton fabric is **durable**, so it is good for children's clothing.

What do YOU have that is made from cotton?

19

Pants and T-shirts are made of cotton fabric. So are blankets and pillowcases. Old **denim** from blue jeans is even used to make dollar bills.

Look around to find things made from cotton.

Nomad Press
A division of Nomad Communications
10 9 8 7 6 5 4 3 2 1

Printed by Regal Printing Limited in China,
June 2011, Job Number 1105034
ISBN: 978-1-936313-92-1

Educational Consultant, Marla Conn

Questions regarding the ordering of this book should be addressed to
Independent Publishers Group
814 N. Franklin St., Chicago, IL 60610
www.ipgbook.com

Nomad Press
2456 Christian St., White River Junction, VT 05001
www.nomadpress.net

Image Credits

©iStockphoto.com/ Sergey Novikov, cover; Rodolfo Arguedas, Sadeugra, title page; Aman Khan, 1;
Olga Popova, 2; Jason Lugo, 3; Burak Demir, 4; Vadim Ponomarenko, 5; Craft Vision, 5; Maria Toutoudaki, 6;
Anna Dedukh, 7; Brazil2, 8; Dave Hughes, 8; Stefanie Timmermann, 9; John A. Meents, 10; Mümin Inan,
Mac Art Grafik, 10; Robert Dant, 11; Shelly Perry, 12; Bela Tiberiu Attl, 12; Nicole S. Young, 13; Gabor Izso,
13; Floortje, 14; Charlotte Lake, 14; Bonnie Jacobs, 15; Skip Odonnell, Odonnell Photograf, 16;
Dmitriy Shironosov, PressFoto, 17; Don Nichols, 18; Mike Sonnenberg, Huron Photo, 19; Antagain, 20.